Perspectives
Trees
Why Do We Need Them?

Series Consultant: Linda Hoyt

Flying Start
to Literacy®

T0359875

Contents

Introduction

Trees – why do we need them?

Did you know that the world would end if there were no trees? So, trees really do mean life! Without them, we would not survive.

But why is this the case? Why are trees so important?

4

Tree story

Every tree has a story, a story about its life cycle.

Read about the life cycle of the maple tree. What does this make you think about?

A maple tree grew tall in the forest.

The tree was a busy place.

A woodpecker pecked for insects that lived beneath the tree's bark.

Squirrels scampered in the tree's branches.

Blue jays flew in
and out of the
tree all day.

A family of
barred owls
looked out from
a hollow high
in the tree's
branches.

One day, lightning struck
the old maple tree.

Down it fell.

Ants built nests
under the bark.

Slugs moved in.

A raccoon built
its den in a hole.

Millipedes liked
the cool, damp
spaces between
the old tree and
the forest floor.

Some animals left,
but new ones came.

After many years, the old tree rotted and crumbled.

Then, one day, in the very place the great old tree once stood, a tiny, new tree sprouted.

And that was the beginning of a new tree story.

Toadstools and mushrooms appeared.

In time, fungi
and moss
covered the tree.

Earthworms
helped turn the
rotting tree into
fine, black soil.

A new maple
tree started to
grow.

Speak out!

Are trees important? Read what these students have to say.

We don't know how much we are harming Earth by cutting down trees. Every day, we cut down more and more trees for farms and to make things such as wooden chairs, tables, paper and even cardboard. We have to make sure that we don't cut down all the trees.

Trees and plants are the start of the food chain, and without them, the circle of life wouldn't work properly. Without plants, there would be no food for the herbivores that provide food for the carnivores.

Trees filter the air we breathe. Humans breathe in oxygen and produce carbon dioxide. Without trees, we would not have enough oxygen in the air to survive. Without air, the human race will cease to exist.

My favourite tree is the weeping willow tree because, when I step through the branches, I feel like I have stepped into a magic kingdom. I imagine there are lots of fairies and small unicorns flying around.

I love where I live

Written by Ally Adams

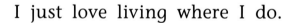

Ally loves the trees around her house, but sometimes, they worry her.

Would you live where Ally lives?

I just love living where I do.

Our house is high on a hill and we can see the ocean in the distance. It can be blue and sparkling or grey and stormy, but it is always wonderful to look at.

All around us are tall trees and they are beautiful. There are all sorts of birds, and some of them will eat special bird food from our hands.

I love living here, but sometimes, it is scary.

In summer, it gets very hot and we worry about bushfires. It can be quiet and still, and then suddenly, we can hear the wind come roaring through the trees. It's the north wind and I don't like it. Lots of the trees around us could catch fire very quickly, so we listen to the radio and make sure that we know if there are any fires nearby.

When strong winds blow, the trees bend, and small branches break off and are blown to the ground. Will any of the trees fall down? Will they fall on our house? My mum and dad always make sure that the trees near us are safe. Sometimes, a tree needs to be cut down because some of its branches are beginning to rot and die, and the tree could fall.

We know that our trees can be dangerous, but we still love living here.

How to write about your opinion

State your opinion

Think about the main question in the introduction on page 4 of this book. What is your opinion?

Research

Look for other information that you need to back up your opinion.

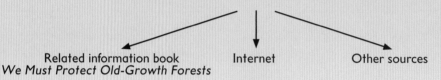

Related information book *We Must Protect Old-Growth Forests*	Internet	Other sources

Make a plan

Introduction

How will you "hook" the reader to get them interested?

Write a sentence that makes your opinion clear.

List reasons to support your opinion.

Support your reason with examples.	Support your reason with examples.	Support your reason with examples.

Conclusion

Write a sentence that makes your opinion clear. Leave your reader with a strong message.

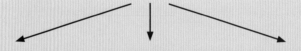

Publish

Publish your writing.

Include some graphics or visual images.